A Blueprint for the Future of Migratory Birds

*Migratory Bird Program
Strategic Plan 2004-2014*

Message from the Assistant Director for Migratory Birds and State Programs

The Migratory Bird Program of the U.S. Fish and Wildlife Service enjoys a rich and successful tradition. It has been instrumental, on its own and with partners, in delivering bird conservation throughout the hemisphere for several decades. It is a critical hub through which much is accomplished.

This strategic plan outlines the future direction of the Migratory Bird Program and how it will continue to contribute to bird conservation in North America and around the world. Like a "blueprint" it lays out the goals and design for a promising future for migratory birds.

This "blueprint" reflects the collective wisdom of many people and groups that care deeply about birds and their habitats. Birds are indicators of the health and quality of our environment and are enjoyed by a large proportion of our citizens. It is critically important for us to better understand the dynamics of those bird populations and habitats that are in trouble and then take actions to intervene strategically and effectively whenever we can. And it is also important to support actions to keep "common birds common."

Clearly, the U.S. Fish and Wildlife Service alone cannot achieve the conservation of migratory birds — it will take the collective and coordinated efforts of thousands of partner organizations and citizens to do this. Birds are everywhere and we all have a responsibility to act on their behalf. As directed by international treaties and domestic legislation, the United States government and its people have called upon the Service to serve as a leader, a catalyst, and a facilitator of local, regional, national, and international partnerships to protect, restore, and manage all native migratory birds for future generations. This plan provides the structure and framework to guide the Service in this all- important effort.

We will use this strategic plan as a guidepost for future funding and policy decisions; however, this plan is both dynamic and evolutionary. We will revise it periodically, with input from our partners, to reflect lessons learned from both our successes and our failures. And we will hold ourselves accountable for results which will add up to a better future for migratory birds and their habitats throughout the hemisphere and beyond.

As you read this plan, please consider how you can contribute to the Vision, Priorities, Goals, and Strategies of the "blueprint." It will take all of us to make it happen. And the beneficiaries will be future generations of citizens who will continue to hear birds singing in the morning; who will delight in seeing a bird in their backyard or along a nature trail; or who will enjoy connecting with nature through a hunting experience.

Let's work together to give birds, and people, a promising future.

Paul R. Schmidt

Paul Schmidt
Assistant Director for Migratory Birds and State Programs
U.S. Fish and Wildlife Service

Table of Contents

Bob Ballou

Propelled by an ancient faith deep within their genes, billions of birds hurdle the globe each season...They are not residents of any single place but of the whole, and their continued survival rests almost entirely within our hands.
Scott Weidensaul

Photos on front cover: Top row: Lesser Scaup, Dave Menke; Prairie Warbler, Steve Maslowski;
Middle row: Hunters, Megan Durham U.S. Fish and Wildlife Service; Earth, NASA/U.S. Fish and Wildlife Service; Birdwatcher, Steve Lewis
Bottom row: Red-footed Booby, Karen Hollingsworth; Bar-tailed Godwit, Tim Bowman
Photo on back cover: Great Egret in tree, Rob Miller
Illustrations by Bob Hines

I. Introduction

Migratory Birds: A Federal Trust Resource

The seasonal ebb and flow of migratory birds is one of the most complex and compelling dramas in the natural world. Driven by a genetic memory millions of years in the making, these animals embark twice each year on long-distance journeys between their breeding areas and wintering grounds. Their travels traverse states, landscapes, and oceans throughout the hemispheres linking the countries, peoples, and ecosystems they visit. The conservation and management of animals capable of such impressive mobility requires strong federal leadership to foster effective partnerships among the many nations, states, provinces, tribes and organizations that are woven together by the flight paths of these remarkable species.

The U.S. Fish and Wildlife Service (Service) is the principal federal agency charged with protecting and enhancing the populations and habitats of more than 800 species of migratory birds that spend all or part of their lives in the United States. The Service is committed to undertaking an unprecedented level of cooperation and coordination to protect and conserve these international treasures.

Birds and People

Because of their ubiquitous and conspicuous presence, migratory birds symbolize America's wildlife experience. Birds enrich human lives in innumerable ways and the loss of bird populations would immeasurably diminish the quality of life for a large segment of the American public. Birds have intrinsic value to people as threads in the earth's ecological tapestry, as pollinators, predators, and prey. Birds are also actively appreciated and enjoyed by millions of people throughout the country.

Nearly 82 million residents of the United States - 39 percent of the adult population - participate in wildlife-related activities, and 64 million of them pursue bird-related recreation, such as birdwatching, backyard bird feeding, hunting, and photography. These citizens substantially contribute to local economies throughout the country by spending nearly $40 billion annually on these pursuits. Experiences range from an annual

Migratory birds are indeed a source of wonder and inspiration. They weave the nations of the globe together as neighbors.
John Turner

The Arctic tern flies over 20,000 miles (35,000 km) every year – roughly the circumference of the Earth – from its arctic tundra breeding grounds via the coast of Africa to Antarctica and back again. It is declining at the southern edge of its breeding range on the Atlantic Coast. /Dave Menke

1

The human race is challenged more than ever before to demonstrate our mastery, not over nature but of ourselves.
Rachel Carson

The Golden-winged Warbler breeds in Ontario and the northern United States and overwinters in Central America and northern South America. It is among a suite of early successional forest species that have shown some of the greatest declines of any landbird habitat group. /Steve Maslowski

duck-hunting trip to enjoying a chickadee at a backyard feeder to watching a pair of red-tailed hawks from a tractor seat. In addition, more than 13,000 subsistence hunters have a long and rich cultural tradition of harvesting birds in rural Alaska. These citizens have every expectation that their children, grandchildren, and great-grandchildren will be able to experience the same wonder and enjoyment of birds in their natural habitats. The Service recognizes that migratory bird conservation and management is ultimately for the benefit of future generations of birds and people, too.

The Challenges of Today

Compared to a century ago, society today faces a more complex set of environmental problems that occur over the entire ranges of migratory birds. Habitat loss and degradation from a burgeoning human population and direct bird mortality attributable to a host of human-caused factors are redefining the challenges of migratory bird conservation in the twenty-first century. Declines in abundance of many landbird, shorebird, and waterbird populations, coupled with exponential growth of some goose populations, are indicative of ecosystems that have been highly altered.

Reductions in habitat quantity and quality, the primary causes of negative population trends in many species, are exacerbated by the direct loss of bird life from an array of external environmental hazards. Despite the banning of DDT, which resulted from Rachel Carson's far-sighted warning of a "silent spring," pesticides and other contaminants continue to poison birds. Numerous other factors such as high predator populations in human-altered ecosystems, invasive species, collisions with human-made structures, and disease outbreaks collectively cause significant migratory bird mortality. Global warming and the demand for water, particularly in the West, are of considerable concern; however their specific effects on bird populations and habitats are as yet unknown.

Birds are the ultimate indicator of environmental quality. Clean air, clean water, and abundant, diverse habitats are essential for birds to continue to survive and flourish. Without a healthy environment, bird populations will diminish and species will disappear, along with the quality of life for people on this planet.

2

Meeting the Challenges

For more than a century, the Service and its predecessors have endeavored to achieve lasting conservation of migratory birds. The Service's efforts have resulted, for example, in the creation of more than 540 national wildlife refuges and wetland management districts as havens for waterfowl, colonial waterbirds, seabirds, shorebirds and landbirds. The Service developed and continues to carry out the longest operating and most comprehensive survey of animal abundance, the Aerial Waterfowl Breeding Ground Population and Habitat Survey. The Service also guided the recovery of endangered species such as the peregrine falcon and brown pelican. In addition, the Service administers two premier continental partnership-based conservation efforts, the North American Waterfowl Management Plan and the North American Wetlands Conservation Act. Through these accomplishments the Service has left a legacy of leadership in twentieth century migratory bird conservation. However, despite these and other successes, the Service now faces a host of challenges to meet the expectations of growing constituencies that often have conflicting priorities for the conservation and management of migratory birds and their habitats.

To surmount the escalating challenges of this century and meet public expectations for migratory bird conservation and management, the Service needs a clear, well-defined blueprint to guide its actions over the next decade. This strategic plan is designed to meet that need over the ten-year period from 2004-2014. Its purpose is to direct the efforts of those Service offices that administer the Migratory Bird Program, including the Office of Migratory Birds and State Programs through the Washington Office Divisions of Migratory Bird Management and Bird Habitat Conservation, seven Regional Migratory Bird and Joint Venture Program Offices, and associated field stations (see Appendix 1).

To develop this strategic plan, the Migratory Bird Program sought the counsel and wisdom of its partners during a two-month consultation in the fall of 2003 and a Migratory Bird Conservation Forum in January 2004 (see Appendix 2). This plan sets a course for the Service to engage existing and new partners in a comprehensive approach that coordinates and integrates partners' efforts across

The future belongs to those who believe in the beauty of their dreams.
Eleanor Roosevelt

Experiencing long-term population declines, the Northern Pintail breeds throughout most of Alaska and Canada southward into the mid-western United States. It over-winters throughout most of the United States south through Mexico to northern South America. /Dave Menke

The U.S. Fish and Wildlife Service's mission is, working with others, to conserve, protect and enhance fish, wildlife, and plants and their habitats for the continuing benefit of the American people.

The Marbled Godwit breeds primarily in the grasslands of the northern Great Plains and winters in large numbers along the coast of southern California and western Mexico. It is one of many grassland breeders threatened by habitat degradation. /Karen Hollingsworth

geographic scales, taxonomic groups, shared habitats and landscapes, and human cultural experiences. The Migratory Bird Program will update this plan in 2008 based on scientific and technical advances, environmental changes, and results achieved.

Every three years, beginning in Fiscal Year 2005, the Migratory Bird Program will develop action plans that describe those specific priority tasks that it will undertake in the short-term to accomplish the long-term goals of this plan. The Service's seven Regional Offices and Washington Office will play important roles in carrying out these actions as well as coordinating and collaborating with partners within and outside the Service. Working with other Service programs, public and private organizations, and individuals is essential to secure a future for migratory birds. State wildlife agencies play special roles by working with the Service to assume co-management responsibilities for migratory birds, in addition to managing the resident game bird species which have been entrusted to their care.

II. Migratory Bird Program Direction

This section presents the overall vision for the Migratory Bird Program which is firmly grounded in the mission of the Service. The vision is followed by a pair of operating principles which underpin the administration of Migratory Bird Program. Following the operating principles are sets of priorities and goals that break down the vision into specific components. The Migratory Bird Program will work to achieve these priorities and goals using implementation strategies in five areas of responsibility, presented in the third section of this plan.

A. Mission of the Service for Migratory Birds

The U.S. Fish and Wildlife Service has the legal mandate and the trust responsibility to maintain healthy migratory bird populations for the benefit of the American public. The Service is authorized by more than 25 primary conventions, treaties, and laws to ensure the conservation of more than 800 species of migratory birds and their habitats (see Appendix 3). Many of the treaties extend beyond the borders of the United States. The Service works with many foreign governments, state and other federal agencies, tribes, non-profit organizations, academic institutions, industry, and private individuals, both within the United States and abroad, to meet these mandates.

B. Vision of the Migratory Bird Program

Through careful management built on solid science and diverse partnerships, the Service and its partners restore and sustain the epic sweep of bird migration and the natural systems on which it depends — fostering a world in which bird populations continue to fulfill their ecological roles while lifting the human spirit and enriching human lives in infinite ways, for generations to come.

C. Operating Principles

To meet the migratory bird conservation challenges of the twenty-first century, the Migratory Bird Program will consistently adhere to the principles of sound science and collaborative partnerships in its migratory bird conservation and management activities.

1. Science

The success of the Service and its partners depends on creating a solid scientific foundation for conserving and managing migratory bird populations. The Migratory Bird Program will strengthen and expand its internal scientific capabilities in monitoring and assessment, as well as increase the use of research results generated by the U.S. Geological Survey (USGS), academic institutions, and others, in an adaptive resource management framework. To realize its vision for migratory bird conservation, the Migratory Bird Program commits to obtaining a more comprehensive understanding of how priority bird populations respond to human caused threats and environmental stressors, such as habitat loss and alteration, and to corrective actions such as habitat restoration and enhancement. Generating and using scientific information within an adaptive

Great things are done by a series of small things brought together.
Vincent Van Gogh

The Wood Thrush has declined significantly across its breeding range since the mid-1960s. Like other deciduous forest habitat specialists, it faces continuing degradation and destruction of both its North American breeding grounds and Central American wintering grounds. /Steve Maslowski

Great discoveries and improvements invariably involve the cooperation of many minds.
Alexander Graham Bell

From Alaskan and eastern Siberian breeding grounds, the Western Sandpiper migrates southeast to wintering areas on both coasts of North and South America. Like many shorebird species, it remains vulnerable because of declining numbers and dependence on a relatively few critical stopover sites, such as the Copper River Delta in Alaska. /Karen Hollingsworth

management context will enable the Service and its partners to make more cost-effective policy, management, and regulatory decisions that meet migratory bird conservation goals and objectives at continental, national, and landscape scales.

2. Partnerships

To achieve our shared migratory bird conservation vision and goals, the Migratory Bird Program will cultivate enduring partnerships. Because migratory birds inhabit a variety of landscapes as they move across state lines and international borders, virtually all nations, organizations, and individuals can influence migratory birds and their habitats. The Migratory Bird Program will take a more active leadership role in coordinating and communicating among all stakeholders to carry out the most comprehensive and cost-effective strategies to protect, restore, and manage migratory birds. A lasting legacy of migratory birds for future generations is only possible through the mutual stewardship that results when partners work together.

D. Program Priorities

The Service and its partners in migratory bird conservation face not only environmental, but also fiscal, technical, and administrative challenges. Therefore, the Migratory Bird Program must use its resources strategically and effectively to realize the far-reaching vision stated in this plan.

With the help of partners and constituents at the Migratory Bird Conservation Forum in January 2004, and during the strategic plan's consultation in the fall of 2003, the Service identified the following top three priorities for the Migratory Bird Program:

- **Address the loss and degradation of migratory bird habitats.**

- **Increase and improve scientific information on migratory bird populations.**

- **Strengthen and expand regional, national, and international partnerships to achieve comprehensive bird conservation.**

The Service will focus its limited resources on the bird species or populations in greatest need of conservation and management. The Migratory Bird Program has developed a list of Birds of Management Concern to provide important focus for the Service's migratory bird conservation efforts over the next ten years and will periodically revise this list to reflect changes in species status (see Appendix 4).

E. Program Goals

To fulfill its many legal responsibilities for migratory bird conservation and to address the mission, vision, and priorities stated above, the Service will expand both the breadth and depth of its Migratory Bird Program to address the full range of species in need of conservation.

The Migratory Bird Program will work to accomplish the following three overarching goals which are stepped down into quantifiable long-term goals and annual performance goals and measures through the process established by the Government Performance and Results Act (GPRA). These goals flow from the Department of the Interior's Strategic Plan and the Fish and Wildlife Service's GPRA Implementation Plan (see Appendix 5).

> **Goal 1: Protect, restore, and manage migratory bird populations to ensure their ecological sustainability and increase their socioeconomic benefits.**
>
> **Goal 2: Protect, restore, and manage migratory bird habitats to ensure long-term sustainability of all migratory bird populations.**
>
> **Goal 3: Improve hunting, birdwatching, and other outdoor bird-related experiences and opportunities, and increase awareness of the value of migratory birds and their habitats for their intrinsic, ecological, recreational and economic significance.**

To work on behalf of the wild is to restore culture.
Gary Snyder

Breeding from Maine north to the arctic, the Common Eider, like other sea ducks, is one of the least well-studied species of waterfowl It is particularly vulnerable to oil spills because it congregates in large, dense, flocks during winter, molting, and migration. /Glen Smart

III. Implementation Strategies

The Migratory Bird Program will achieve its vision, priorities, and goals by implementing strategies in the following five areas of responsibility:

A. Population Monitoring, Assessment, and Management
B. Habitat Conservation
C. Permits and Regulations
D. Consultation, Cooperation, Communication
E. Recreation

In addition, other programs of the Service, including the National Wildlife Refuge System, Endangered Species, International Affairs, and Fisheries and Habitat Conservation programs are committed to helping achieve Migratory Bird Program goals though their own strategic contributions (see Appendix 6).

A. Population Monitoring, Assessment, and Management

Information on the population status and trends of migratory birds is required to comply with mandates in the various migratory bird treaties and other legislation (e.g., the Migratory Bird Treaty Act and the Fish and Wildlife Conservation Act). Because most migratory birds range widely over their annual cycles, an accurate assessment of status, including distribution, population abundance, and trends, requires long-term monitoring over broad geographic scales — regional, national, continental, and range-wide. Monitoring is also needed to evaluate the effects of management and conservation activities and human and environmental factors on bird demographics and distribution. The Service, other federal and state agencies, and non-governmental organizations conduct surveys that greatly contribute to understanding bird populations. The Service has the added responsibility for providing an international perspective to migratory bird assessment and management.

The Migratory Bird Program has come close to fulfilling this responsibility for some species of waterfowl, a group for which broad-scale monitoring programs have been in place for many years. However, information is insufficient for many other migratory birds, hindering the Service's ability to clearly determine population status and reasonably predict the outcome of management and conservation activities and environmental changes. With its partners, the Service will implement, coordinate, and facilitate robust, sustainable range-wide surveys, and develop and improve monitoring objectives and protocols necessary to assess migratory bird abundances, distributions, trends, causes of population conditions, and responses to management and conservation activities.

Strategies for Monitoring:

A-1: Establish clear, quantifiable, and measurable objectives for all survey and monitoring projects undertaken or funded by the Migratory Bird Program.

A-2: Complete a review of all Service supported migratory bird surveys as a first step toward identifying gaps, reducing redundancy, and increasing efficiency.

A-3: Evaluate the design and operation of Service supported migratory bird surveys relative to objectives, and institute improvements or discontinue surveys where appropriate.

A-4: Facilitate periodic, independent evaluations of survey objectives, designs, operations, data management, and analyses and reporting of survey and assessment information, including critiques of data coverage and quality, for all Service supported migratory bird surveys.

A-5: Work with partners to develop and implement statistically rigorous surveys and range-wide monitoring programs for Birds of Management Concern.

A-6: Establish formal, periodic consultation processes with the states, flyway councils, and other partners to determine regional and national priority survey, monitoring, and management issues for game and nongame migratory birds.

A-7: Provide private and public land managers with technical assistance in selecting and implementing appropriate bird survey and monitoring techniques.

Strategies for Analytical Support and Information Dissemination:

A-8: Increase capabilities for analytical support, including survey design, data storage and management, and analysis.

A-9: Create a dynamic, user-friendly information and communication system to provide universal access to survey data and analysis.

A-10: Report regularly on the status and trends of bird populations based on information derived from monitoring and research programs.

Strategies for Research:

A-11: Support research aimed at improving the effectiveness and efficiency of monitoring protocols, increasing power, precision and accuracy of analyses, and expanding the availability and utility of data.

A-12: Support range-wide research on factors that directly affect migratory bird populations, such as disease, predation, competition, brood parasitism, environmental factors, and human-caused mortality.

A-13: Support range-wide research on factors that affect bird populations through reducing habitat quality and quantity, such as invasive species, agricultural and other land use practices, and habitat fragmentation.

A-14: Evaluate the effectiveness of management actions and develop or refine best management practices for migratory birds using an adaptive management framework.

Strategies for Population Management:

A-15: Work with other nations, flyways, and bird conservation initiatives to develop explicit, unambiguous management objectives for Birds of Management Concern.

A-16: Within an adaptive management framework, undertake conservation and management actions, consistent with bird conservation plans, to achieve desired abundance levels or to reintroduce desired species.

A-17: Provide federal land management agencies, states, and other land and water management partners with technical support necessary to undertake conservation and management actions consistent with bird conservation plans.

A.18: Periodically review and adjust desired population levels and objectives based on the results of research, monitoring, and assessment.

A-19: Based on valid scientific data, reduce to acceptable levels the abundances of migratory bird species that create economic and ecological damage and human health and safety concerns.

A-20: Identify and implement actions to respond to threats to migratory birds from diseases and invasive species, including alien wildlife.

A-21: Support efforts by the USGS National Wildlife Health Center and other partners to identify, study, and address traditional and emerging bird disease problems such as botulism, avian cholera, Newcastle disease, and West Nile virus.

A-22: Implement and improve surveys to measure subsistence harvest of migratory birds in Alaska, and conduct appropriate analyses to assess likely population impacts of that harvest.

The Swainson's Hawk migrates over 6,000 miles (10,000 km) every spring and fall between its North American breeding grounds and South American wintering grounds. It is threatened by habitat destruction, a reduction in its prey, and pesticide use. /Karen Hollingsworth

B. Habitat Conservation

Protection, restoration, and enhancement of terrestrial, aquatic and marine habitats, landscapes, and seascapes are crucial to restore and sustain migratory bird populations. Since its inception, the Service has placed a premium on providing high quality habitats for migratory birds, and traditionally the National Wildlife Refuge System and the Partners for Fish and Wildlife Programs have been the cornerstones of this effort. In addition, the Migratory Bird Program administers national and international programs that implement the North American Wetlands Conservation Act, Neotropical Migratory Bird Conservation Act, and the Migratory Bird Hunting and Conservation Stamp Act. The Migratory Bird Program also supports habitat joint ventures, which are regional, landscape-oriented public-private partnerships dedicated to conserving habitat for birds. Together, these programs serve as catalysts for habitat conservation and management throughout the hemisphere. The contribution of private landowners, state and other federal agencies, tribes, non-profit organizations, corporations, and academia to bird habitat conservation is essential to meet migratory bird goals and objectives and, through these programs, the Service works closely with these partners.

Despite the great successes of these and other Service habitat programs, many migratory bird habitats remain imperiled. The Migratory Bird Program will continue to develop national and international partnerships to improve and expand efforts to address these threats. Integral to this effort is the development of scientific tools such as modeling and geographic information systems that integrate information on habitat and landscape conditions with demographic data to produce biologically-based landscape designs that meet the needs of multiple species. By developing these tools and increasing the technical assistance capabilities of the Migratory Bird Program, the Service and its partners can more effectively protect, restore, and manage sustainable habitats for migratory birds.

Strategies for Biological Planning:

B-1: Work with partners range-wide to establish habitat conservation objectives for Birds of Management Concern through existing bird conservation planning efforts.

B-2: Work with partners range-wide to integrate migratory bird population and habitat data using biologically-based geospatial planning tools to create sustainable landscape designs for Birds of Management Concern.

Strategies for Conservation Delivery:

B-3: Protect, restore and manage priority terrestrial, aquatic, and marine habitats for birds through the North American Wetlands Conservation Act, Neotropical Migratory Bird Conservation Act, Migratory Bird Hunting and Conservation Stamp Act, and other appropriate funding opportunities.

B-4: Give priority in grant and other funding programs to projects that are designed to achieve population and habitat objectives stated in bird conservation plans and sustainable landscape designs for Birds of Management Concern.

B-5: Participate in promotion, delivery, and evaluation of non-Service habitat conservation programs (e.g., U.S. Department of Agriculture's Conservation Reserve and Wetland Reserve Program and the National Oceanic and Atmospheric Administration's National Marine Sanctuary Program) that have the potential to affect the quantity and quality of migratory bird habitat.

Strategies for Technical Assistance:

B-6: Coordinate with other Service habitat programs (e.g., Endangered Species, National Wildlife Refuge System, and Fisheries and Habitat Conservation Programs) by communicating bird population and habitat requirements to maximize the benefits of these programs to migratory birds, as required by Executive Order 13186 (see Appendix 6).

B-7: Provide technical assistance to Service field stations and private and public partners on the most effective protection, restoration and management practices for migratory bird habitats.

B-8: Coordinate with public and private partners that manage resources, such as agricultural land, timber, grasslands, fisheries, and energy, by communicating migratory bird requirements to minimize the adverse impacts and maximize the benefits of these programs to migratory birds.

Strategies for Habitat Assessment:

B-9: Work with partners to track changes in migratory bird habitats across the entire ranges of Birds of Management Concern.

B-10: Work with partners to coordinate population monitoring with habitat monitoring, where necessary, to develop sustainable landscape designs for Birds of Management Concern.

B-11: Promote research to better assess landscape changes and their impacts on Birds of Management Concern at local, regional and continental scales.

C. Permits and Regulations

Under the authorities of the Migratory Bird Treaty Act and the Bald and Golden Eagle Protection Act, the Service regulates the take of migratory birds for hunting, rehabilitation, preventing depredation, scientific collection, religious use, and other purposes. Regulating take is a primary and traditional Service activity that uses monitoring and assessment information to manage migratory bird populations. Overall, the Service's challenge is to balance the take of migratory birds with international, national and regional commitments to conserve them.

Each year the Service conducts a well-defined cycle of procedures and events, including public consultation, which results in rules governing annual sport and subsistence harvest for migratory game bird species. For other direct take activities, the Migratory Bird Program issues thousands of permits that regulate the number and species of birds that can be taken. Permits provide a means to balance use and conservation, and allow the Service to monitor activities to determine how they affect migratory birds. The Service will continue to improve the hunting and permits regulations processes to better serve migratory birds and the public. For example, through Adaptive Harvest Management the Service applies the best available science to provide hunting opportunities consistent with established harvest objectives, while considering the status and long-term conservation of migratory game birds. The Service's Law Enforcement program also plays a critical role in ensuring that migratory bird hunting and other forms of take are conducted within the bounds of the law.

The Migratory Bird Program also works with other Service programs in the review, consultation, and permitting process for federal land management activities and for private activities requiring federal permits and licenses. These programs work together to conserve wildlife in accordance with laws, while streamlining the permitting process to help the public.

Executive Order 13186, *Responsibilities of Federal Agencies to Protect Migratory Birds* directs federal agencies whose actions have a measurable negative impact on migratory bird populations to develop Memoranda of Understanding with the Service to promote the conservation of migratory birds. This Order will have important implications to migratory bird conservation in the coming years.

Strategies for Permits:

C-1: Implement actions outlined in the Service's document *Leaving a Lasting Legacy: Permits as a Conservation Tool* to streamline the migratory bird permit program, provide better customer service, and support conservation (see Appendix 7).

C-2: In cooperation with partners, develop and implement biologically sound permits, regulations, policies, and procedures to effectively manage and assess the take of migratory birds, while decreasing the administrative burden for permit applicants.

C-3: Implement the recommendations in the Service's Permits Workload Analysis to provide resources to meet customer needs.

Strategies for Hunting Regulations:

C-4: Continue to implement and improve an objective, streamlined process for establishing annual hunting regulations and strengthen the working relationships with flyway councils and individual states.

C-5: Enhance the use of Adaptive Harvest Management as an effective approach to managing migratory game bird harvests.

C-6: Continue to provide an effective forum for public review and comment during the development of annual hunting regulations.

C-7: Work with the Alaska Migratory Bird Co-management Council to provide for regulated spring and summer subsistence harvest of migratory birds consistent with bird conservation goals, remaining cognizant of the desires of other stakeholders and user-groups.

C-8: Work with Native American tribes to improve the process for establishing annual hunting regulations.

Strategies for Other Legal Compliance:

C-9: Develop and implement Memoranda of Understanding with other federal agencies to promote bird conservation under Executive Order 13186 through adoption of processes and measures that avoid or minimize the negative impacts of agency actions on migratory birds.

C-10: Work with the Service's Office of Law Enforcement and state and tribal law enforcement officials to ensure compliance with the laws and international conventions applicable to migratory birds.

D. Consultation, Cooperation, and Communication

The Migratory Bird Program works with partners throughout the ranges of migratory birds — at the local, state, regional, national, and international levels — to achieve a biologically based, landscape-oriented approach to migratory bird conservation. The Migratory Bird Program is committed to strengthening its tools of consultation, cooperation, and communication to increase and energize its partnerships. The Migratory Bird Program supports habitat joint ventures which are regional, landscape-oriented partnerships working to conserve habitat for birds in North America. Through species joint ventures the Migratory Bird Program cooperates with international partners to answer biological and ecological questions regarding individual waterfowl species or populations. The Service works closely with the flyway councils which deal with a variety of migratory bird management issues at the state, provincial, and flyway scales, including the development of hunting regulations.

The Migratory Bird Program serves as a focal point for developing and implementing regional, national, and continental bird conservation plans, including the North American Waterfowl Management Plan, Partners in Flight Landbird Conservation Plans, the U.S. Shorebird Conservation Plan, the North American Waterbird Conservation Plan, and migratory game bird management plans for waterfowl, woodcock, and doves developed by the flyway councils. These plans present population and habitat goals for priority species and have been developed by coalitions of federal, state, and provincial agencies, tribal entities, foreign governments, non-governmental organizations, industry, academia, and private individuals.

The Service also supports the North American Bird Conservation Initiative (NABCI) which provides a forum for state, regional, national, and international organizations and bird initiatives to coordinate their efforts to increase resources and expand partnerships to deliver integrated bird conservation. NABCI is facilitating partners' efforts to integrate bird conservation plans, develop comprehensive, sustainable landscape designs for birds, and carry out all-bird conservation through regional partnerships, such as joint ventures. For example, NABCI developed and approved Bird Conservation Regions (BCRs) as ecological units within which planning and implementation can occur. The Service will continue to support partnerships at every scale that advance an integrated and comprehensive approach to bird conservation.

Strategies for Coordination:

D-1: Actively support and participate with partners in developing, implementing, and evaluating bird conservation plans at appropriate geographic scales.

D-2: Coordinate bird conservation planning efforts with other ongoing planning efforts, including State Comprehensive Wildlife Conservation Plans.

D-3: Work with partner agencies and organizations to obtain additional funding for all-bird conservation and to leverage resources towards agreed upon goals identified in bird conservation plans and sustainable landscape designs.

D-4: Coordinate bird planning and implementation efforts with Canada, Mexico, Central and South America, the Caribbean, and other nations that share migratory birds.

D-5: Support NABCI efforts to facilitate and coordinate integrated bird conservation planning and implementation at the international, national, regional, and state levels.

D-6: Expand existing or create new habitat joint ventures to encompass all bird habitats (terrestrial, aquatic, and marine) in North America, and initiate and strengthen similar partnerships beyond North America.

D-7: Provide technical assistance to partner agencies and organizations through federal project reviews and other means to integrate migratory bird conservation objectives into their project planning and implementation.

D-8: Coordinate and communicate with the USGS Biological Resources Discipline to obtain directed research and development information and technical assistance on migratory birds and their habitats and factors affecting them.

D-9: Strengthen range-wide migratory bird management by improving international partnerships among Migratory Bird Treaty Act nations and other nations within flyways used by migratory birds.

Strategies for Consultation and Technical Assistance:

D-10: Assist other nations and U.S. partners in assessing the status of migratory birds, identifying important habitats, and developing strategies to conserve shared resources through national and international grant programs and direct technical assistance.

D-11: Provide technical assistance to other Service programs (e.g., National Wildlife Refuges, International Conservation, Endangered Species and Fisheries and Habitat Conservation) to increase their ability to meet trust responsibilities for migratory bird conservation.

D-12: Provide information to private landowners to assist them in protecting and restoring bird populations and habitats on a voluntary basis.

D-13: Provide technical assistance to industry on ways to avoid or minimize impacts of communications towers, wind turbines, fishing bycatch, and other hazards to migratory birds and recognize positive industry efforts that result in increased conservation (e.g., communications industry).

Strategies for Communications and Outreach:

D-14: Review and expand existing and develop new products, programs, and venues that increase awareness of the value of conserving migratory birds and their habitats (e.g., International Migratory Bird Day and Urban Conservation Treaties for Migratory Birds).

D-15: Promote and expand existing programs that increase awareness of the value of comprehensive, integrated approaches to bird conservation that conserve all priority bird species across geopolitical boundaries, taxonomic groups, and sociocultural divides.

D-16: Increase sales of the Migratory Bird Hunting and Conservation Stamp (i.e., Federal Duck Stamp) by expanding public awareness of this program, beyond its traditional hunting constituency, as the most direct way for citizens to protect migratory bird habitat.

D-17: Increase student and school participation in the Junior Duck Stamp Program and strengthen its educational content by incorporating its curriculum into national and state science and art education standards.

D-18: Increase involvement of organizations and individuals representing ethnic and culturally diverse communities in bird conservation efforts.

D-19: Take actions to ensure the nation's students are knowledgeable about the conservation needs of migratory birds and to instill stewardship of natural resources by promoting awareness, appreciation, and knowledge of birds through such programs as Shorebird Sister Schools and Flying WILD, which is sponsored by the President's Council for Environmental Education.

E. Recreation

Millions of Americans enjoy observing, photographing, and hunting migratory birds in their natural habitats. The Service is committed to providing U.S. citizens with quality outdoor recreational opportunities involving migratory birds by conserving these species and their habitats. By working with the National Wildlife Refuge System, the Migratory Bird Program is helping to improve migratory bird recreation on national wildlife refuge and other Service lands. Through other partnerships, the Migratory Bird Program will promote and improve bird-related recreational opportunities for people on other public and private lands.

Providing the public with opportunities for quality recreation promotes a strong conservation ethic. By participating in quality recreation involving experiential education (e.g., nature studies and work on conservation projects) and individual reflection (e.g., birdwatching and hunting) citizens develop a deep sense of wonder and appreciation for the natural world as well as a sense of responsibility for protecting and restoring the earth's community of life for future generations.

Strategies for Improving Recreational Opportunities:

E-1: Work with the National Wildlife Refuge System to actively implement the provisions of the Refuge Improvement Act to improve the quantity and quality of migratory bird-related recreation on National Wildlife Refuge System lands, as compatible with refuge goals and authorizing legislation.

E-2: Actively support state efforts to provide bird-related recreation through the Service's Federal Assistance programs, including the State Wildlife Grants program.

E-3: With partners, identify and implement projects and programs to improve the quality of hunting, birdwatching, and other recreational opportunities related to migratory birds.

Strategies for Increasing Public Awareness:

E-4: With partners, identify and promote recreational opportunities associated with migratory birds, such as hunting and birdwatching.

E-5: Open dialogs with federal, regional, state and local managers of land and water resources to encourage recreational opportunities related to birds.

E-6: Work with birding industries (e.g., optics manufacturers and birdseed companies), rehabilitators, and other stakeholders to create new partnerships and venues that increase public awareness of non-consumptive bird recreation and bird conservation (e.g., birding festivals, trails, and conferences).

E-7: Maintain and expand existing conservation partnerships with hunters and the hunting industry to increase awareness of hunting opportunities and the importance of bird conservation.

U.S. Fish and Wildlife Service

When we see land as a community to which we belong, we may begin to use it with love and respect.
Aldo Leopold

Megan Durham/U.S. Fish and Wildlife Service

14

Acknowledgments

Gratitude goes to the many people who contributed to the development of this strategic plan including more than 200 commenters and the 65 Service employees and partners who participated in the Migratory Bird Conservation Forum at the National Conservation Training Center (NCTC) in Shepherdstown, West Virginia on January 20-22, 2004. The writing team for this strategic plan included Roxanne Bogart, John Christian, Bob Blohm, Cyndi Perry, Seth Mott, Bob Ford, and Brad Andres, with editorial assistance from Steve Lewis and Scott Schwenk. Thanks to members of the Migratory Bird Strategic Plan Steering Committee for leading the way for migratory bird conservation in the twenty-first century: Paul Schmidt, Brian Millsap, David Smith, Doug Alcorn, John Christian, Paul Gertler, Roxanne Bogart, Phil Million, Greg Knadle, Anne Hoover, and Chris McKay. Special thanks to Genevieve Pullis for helping to organize and coordinate the Conservation Forum. Thanks to Janet Ady and her staff at NCTC and David J. Case for their help in making the Conservation Forum possible. Gratitude goes to members of Comment Review Team, especially Genevieve Pullis and Shauna Hanisch. Special thanks to Beth Andujar and Harish Bellary for helping to create the migratory bird strategic plan web pages, e-mail user groups, and comments database. Thanks to the many staff of the Migratory Bird Program throughout the country who provided valuable comments and helped pull together information for this document. Special thanks to Scott Weidensaul for lifting our spirits at the Conservation Forum and for crafting an inspirational vision worthy of the remarkable species we all seek to conserve.

Though absent from much of its historic range, the Whooping Crane has been brought back from the brink of extinction through decades of research and management. /John Christian

Introduction to Appendices

The following appendices provide additional information on the Service's Migratory Bird Program and links to important resources that explain and guide the Program's conservation efforts. Readers are encouraged to visit the following site for more information: http://migratorybirds.fws.gov/mbstratplan/mbstratplan.htm

Appendix 1: Organization and Budget Structure of the Migratory Bird Program

The Service's Migratory Bird Program has primary responsibility for the conservation and management of migratory birds and their habitats. Essential staff and funding support come from other parts of the Service that deal routinely with this trust resource, including the National Wildlife Refuge System, Law Enforcement, International Affairs, Fisheries and Habitat Conservation, and Endangered Species.

The leader of the Migratory Bird Program is the Assistant Director for Migratory Birds and State Programs located in Washington, D.C. There are four program components under the Assistant Director: the Division of Migratory Bird Management (DMBM), the Division of Bird Habitat Conservation (DBHC), the Division of Federal Aid, and the Office of Aviation Management. The Migratory Bird Permit Program is managed by DMBM. The Federal Duck Stamp Office is managed by DBHC. The primary functions of the Washington Office staff include legislative, regulatory, budget and policy development, and program guidance.

The Migratory Bird Program is implemented on the ground by the Assistant Regional Directors for Migratory Birds and State Programs through seven Regional Offices and associated field stations with programs for Migratory Bird Management and Joint Ventures. Research support to the Migratory Bird Program within the Department of Interior is provided by the Biological Resources Discipline of the U.S. Geological Survey located in Reston, Virginia and associated regional offices, science centers, and cooperative research units.

The Migratory Bird Program budget structure contains five components for appropriations and execution processes referred to as subactivities: (1) Conservation and Monitoring, (2) Permits, (3) North American Waterfowl Management Plan (Joint Ventures), (4) North American Wetlands Conservation Act and (5) Neotropical Migratory Bird Conservation Act. Annual budgets are structured along subactivity lines. Each component of the budget is justified and allocated independently of the other.

Regional allocation estimates for each subactivity are determined following decisions by the Office of Management and Budget on the President's Budget request level. Budget allocation estimates are displayed in the Congressional District Report by state and congressional district and published as part of the annual President's Budget Justification (Green Book).

Visit the following link to see the Fiscal Year 2005 Migratory Bird Budget Justification:
http://budget.fws.gov/fy%202005%20GB/0602%20mb.pdf

Appendix 2: Public Comment Process and Evolution of the Migratory Bird Strategic Plan

- The draft "Blueprint" document underwent a two-month public review from August to October 2003.

- Comments were solicited during Director William's speech at the annual meetings of the International Association of Fish and Wildlife Agencies in September 2003, in letters to state directors, through e-mails to the bird conservation community, and on the strategic plan webpage on the Service's web site.

- A nine-person Comment Review Team comprised of Service employees from various Regions and programs was established to review and summarize comments received during the partner consultation.

- The consultation resulted in 217 comments received from Service employees and partners.

- Breakdown of affiliations of commenters:
  - 29% non-governmental organizations
  - 25% private citizens
  - 15% state agencies
  - 12% other Federal agencies
  - 11% Service employees
  - 5% for-profit organizations
  - 3% academia

- A majority of the commenters expressed appreciation for the development of a strategic plan, thought the plan was well-written and comprehensive, and showed support for the plan's vision and strategies.

- Of the 25 states that commented, 23 explicitly stated support, agreement, or appreciation for the plan and none expressed lack of support.

- Many states wished for more detailed objectives, continued emphasis on partnerships, and expanded Service leadership in migratory bird conservation.

- Many commenters felt that specific direction in the form of objectives and priorities was missing from the plan.

- Commenters expressed differences of opinion about what should be the Service's focus in migratory bird conservation (e.g., ecological vs. utilitarian values and game vs. nongame).

- Many commenters were concerned that adequate funding is not available to implement the plan and many stated a need to develop ways for non-hunters to provide financial support to migratory bird programs.

- Five high priority areas emerged from the comments:
  - Protect and restore bird habitats (#1)
  - Maintain viable bird populations
  - Conduct science and research
  - Provide leadership for all-bird conservation
  - Stimulate and facilitate partnerships

- In January 2004 at the National Conservation Training Center, the Migratory Bird Program sponsored a Conservation Forum attended by 65 Service employees and partners to discuss the draft "Blueprint."

To see a summary of partner responses, visit http://migratorybirds.fws.gov/mbstratplan/responses.htm

Appendix 3: Primary International Conventions and Major Domestic Legislation for the Conservation of Migratory Birds and their Habitats in the United States

YEAR	AUTHORITY
1900	Lacey Act (Amended 1981)
1913	Weeks-McLean Law (Migratory Bird Conservation Act 1913)
1916	Convention for the Protection of Migratory Birds (Canada)
1918	Migratory Bird Treaty Act
1929	Migratory Bird Conservation Act
1934	Migratory Bird Hunting and Conservation Stamp Act (Duck Stamp Act)
1936	Migratory Bird Convention with Mexico (amended 1972)
1940	Pan American (or Western Hemisphere) Convention
1940	Bald Eagle Protection Act
1956	Waterfowl Depredations Prevention Act
1961	Wetlands Loan Act of 1961 (Amended 1969, 1976)
1972	Migratory Bird Convention with Japan
1972	Convention on Wetlands of International Importance Especially as Waterfowl Habitats (RAMSAR)
1973	Endangered Species Act (ESA)
1973	Convention on International Trade in Endangered Species of Wild Fauna and Flora (CITES)
1976	Migratory Bird Convention with the Union of Soviet Socialist Republics
1978	Antarctic Conservation Act
1980	Fish and Wildlife Conservation Act (Amended 1988, 1989)
1982	Convention on Conservation of Antarctic Living Marine Resources
1986	Emergency Wetlands Resources Act
1987	Driftnet Impact Monitoring, Assessment, and Control Act of 1987
1989	North American Wetlands Conservation Act (NAWCA)
1990	Coastal Wetlands Planning, Protection and Restoration Act
1992	Wild Bird Conservation Act
2000	Neotropical Migratory Bird Conservation Act
2001	Responsibilities of Federal Agencies to Protect Migratory Birds (Executive Order 13186)

To see an overview of primary authorities, visit
http://migratorybirds.fws.gov/mbstratplan/Legalauthamend.pdf

To see a list of secondary authorities, visit
http://migratorybirds.fws.gov/mbstratplan/LegalAuthorities.pdf

Appendix 4: Birds of Management Concern

Birds of Management Concern (BMC) are a subset of the species protected by the Migratory Bird Treaty Act (see 50 CFR 10.13) which pose special management challenges because of a variety of factors (e.g., too few, too many, conflicts with human interests, societal demands). The Migratory Bird Program will place priority emphasis on these birds during the next ten years. The BMC list of 412 species, subspecies, or populations comprises five categories of migratory birds:

(1) birds listed as endangered or threatened under the Endangered Species Act (62),

(2) nongame birds that have been determined to be of conservation concern due to declining populations and other factors (as published in *Birds of Conservation Concern 2002*; 247 including all National, Regional, and Bird Conservation Region species),

(3) game birds that are below desired condition* (35),

(4) game birds that are at or above desired condition** (60), and

(5) birds that are considered overabundant in part or all of their range and thus potentially damaging to natural ecosystems or human interests (8).

The BMC list will be updated periodically to reflect changes in the status of these species or populations. Performance goals and measures have been developed that address the status of these species, subspecies, or populations.

To see the list of Birds of Management Concern, visit
http://migratorybirds.fws.gov/mbstratplan/GPRAMBSpecies.pdf

*Game Birds Below Desired Conditions (GBBDC) are species whose populations are below long-term averages or management goals, or for which there is evidence of declining population trends.

**Game Birds Above Desired Conditions (GBADC) are species whose populations are at or above long-term averages or management goals, or for which there is evidence of increasing population trends.

Appendix 5: Department of the Interior Strategic Plan and GPRA goals

The Government Performance and Results Act (GPRA) mandates that all federal agencies set long-term and annual goals, measure performance, and report on the degree to which goals are met. The three overarching goals of the Migratory Bird Program's strategic plan flow from the Department of the Interior (DOI) Draft Strategic Plan for 2004-2008 and the Draft Fish and Wildlife Service Operational Performance Plan.

The Migratory Bird Program supports the following goals in the DOI strategic plan:

(1) Resource Protection – Biological Communities, Strategy 2, targeted at sustaining biological communities on DOI managed and influenced lands and waters;

(2) Resource Protection – Biological Communities, Strategy 3, targeted at increasing information and knowledge necessary for decision making;

(3) Resource Protection – Cultural and Heritage Resources, Strategy 1, targeted at increasing the knowledge base of cultural and heritage resources managed by DOI; and

(4) Recreation Strategy 1 targeted at increasing the quality of recreational activities involving DOI managed resources, and Strategy 2 targeted at providing effective interpretation and education programs.

The three overarching goals of *A Blueprint for the Future of Migratory Birds* are further stepped down into quantifiable long-term goals and annual performance goals and measures. The Service will report on progress made in achieving these goal and performance measure targets which are available at the following website links:

To see the Migratory Bird Management Division's GPRA goals, visit
http://migratorybirds.fws.gov/mbstratplan/MBFY2004GPRA.pdf

To see the Division of Bird Habitat Conservation's GPRA goals, visit,
http://migratorybirds.fws.gov/mbstratplan/DBHCFY2004GPRA.pdf

Appendix 6: Summary of the Director's Order for Migratory Bird Conservation

In March 2004, a Director's Order (DO) was issued to provide guidance for Service programs on the management and conservation of migratory birds. This DO was developed in accordance with Executive Order (EO) 13186, *Responsibilities of Federal Agencies to Protect Migratory Birds*. The purpose of the DO is to minimize the potential adverse effects of migratory bird take, with the goal of striving to eliminate take, while implementing our mission.

Executive Order 13186, signed on January 10, 2001, directs federal agencies whose actions could have a measurable negative impact on migratory bird populations to develop Memoranda of Understanding (MOUs) with the Service to promote conservation of migratory birds. In addition, the EO calls on federal agencies to take reasonable steps that include restoring and enhancing habitat, incorporating migratory bird conservation into planning processes, promoting research and information exchange, providing training and visitor education, and developing partnerships beyond agency boundaries.

The DO describes how the Service will implement the EO 13186 with respect to its own programs and lists specific strategies for individual programs. Continued intra-Service coordination is essential to maximize the benefits of these programs to migratory bird conservation. The Service is developing a web page that will provide an overview of related activities and individual program strategies that the Service will undertake to fulfill its responsibilities under the DO.

The Migratory Bird Program strategies laid out in this plan, coupled with the DO strategies from other Service programs, constitute the Service's overall commitment to migratory bird conservation.

To see Executive Order 13186 and the Director's Order, visit
http://migratorybirds.fws.gov/mbstratplan/EO.pdf

Appendix 7: *Leaving a Lasting Legacy: Permits as a Conservation Tool*

As authorized by the Migratory Bird Treaty Act, the Service issues permits to qualified applicants for the following types of activities: falconry, raptor propagation, scientific collecting, special purposes (e.g., rehabilitation, education, migratory game bird propagation, and salvage), take of depredating birds, taxidermy, and waterfowl sale and disposal. Migratory bird permit policy is developed by the Division of Migratory Bird Management and the permits themselves are issued by the Regional Bird Permit Offices. The regulations governing migratory bird permits can be found in 50 CFR part 13 (General Permit Procedures) and 50 CFR part 21 (Migratory Bird Permits).

In addition to permits issued by the Migratory Bird Program, the Service also issues permits through its Endangered Species, International Affairs, and Law Enforcement programs. In 2002, the Service developed a vision and action plan, *Leaving a Lasting Legacy: Permits as a Conservation Tool*, for its various permit programs to promote long-term conservation of animals, plants, and their habitats, and encourage joint stewardship with others. This document can be viewed at:
http://library.fws.gov/IA_Pubs/permits_legacy02.pdf, or go to http://permits.fws.gov, for more information on the Service's permit program.

U.S Fish and Wildlife Service
Migratory Birds and State Programs
4401 North Fairfax Drive, MBSP-4000
Arlington, Virginia 22203
http://birds.fws.gov/